STICKBALL ON 88th STREET

Also by Willis Barnstone

POETRY
From This White Island (Bookman, 1960)
A Day in the Country (Harper & Row, 1971)
New Faces of China (Indiana, 1972)
China Poems(Missouri, 1977)
A Snow Salmon Reached the Andes Lake(Curbstone, 1980)
Five A.M. in Beijing (Sheep Meadow), 1987)
Funny Ways of Staying Alive: Poems and Ink Drawings (New England, 1993)
The Secret Reader: 501 Sonnets (New England, 1996)
Algebra of Night: New & Selected Poems 1948-1998 (Sheep Meadow, 1998)
Life Watch (BOA Editions, 2003)
Café de l'Aube à Paris / Dawn Café in Paris (Sheep Meadow, 2011)

MEMOIR
With Borges on an Ordinary Evening in Buenos Aires (Illinois, 1993)
Sunday Morning in Fascist Spain: A European Memoir (1948–1953)(Southern Illinois)
We Jews and Blacks, with Poems by YusefKomunyakaa (Indiana, 2004)

LITERARY CRITICISM
The Poetics of Ecstasy: from Sappho to Borges (Holmes & Meier, 1983)
The Poetics of Translation: History, Theory, Practice (Yale. 1993)

RELIGIOUS SCRIPTURES
The Other Bible (HarperSan Francisco, 1984)
The Apocalypse: Book of Revelation (New Directions, 2000)
The Gnostic Bible (with Marvin Meyer, Shambhala Books, 2003)
The Restored New Testament (WW Norton, 2009)
Essential Gnostic Scriptures (Shambhala, 2010)

TRANSLATIONS & ANTHLOGIES
Greek Lyric Poetry (Bantam Classics, 1962)
Modern European Poetry (Bantam Classics, 1967)
Concrete Poetry, with Mary Ellen Solt (Indiana, 1969).
Eighteen Texts: Writings by Contemporary Greek Authors (Harvard, 1972)
The Poems of Saint John of the Cross (New Directions, 1972)
The Poems of Sappho (Doubleday Anchor, 1975)
A Book of Women Poets from Antiquity, with Aliki Barnstone (Schocken, 1980)
Laughing Lost in the Mountains: Poems of Wang Wei, with Tony Barnstone
    (New England, 1992)
The Literatures of Asia, Africa, and Latin America, with Tony Barnstone
    (Prentice Hall, 1998)
To Touch the Sky: Spiritual, Mystical, and Philosophical Poems
    (New Directions, New York, 1999)
Sonnets to Orpheus by Rainer Maria Rilke (Shambhala, 2004)
Border of a Dream: Selected Poems of Antonio Machado (Copper Canyon, 2004)
The Poems of Mao Zedong (California, 2008)
Love Poems by Pedro Salinas (Chicago, 2010)

STICKBALL ON 88th STREET

poems by

Willis Barnstone

RED HEN PRESS | Pasadena, California

Stickball on 88ᵗʰ Street

Copyright © 2011 by Willis Barnstone

Illustrations by Karmen Effenberger Copyright © 2011
Book layout by Marcus Slater

Library of Congress Cataloging-in-Publication Data
Barnstone, Willis, 1927-
  Stickball on 88th Street : poems / from Willis Barnstone. —1st ed.
    p. cm.
  ISBN 978-1-59709-477-1
  1. City and town life—New York (State)—New York—Poetry. 2. Children—
New York (State)—New York—Poetry. I. Title.
  PS3552.A722S8 2011
  811'.54—dc22

                        2011015980

The Los Angeles County Arts Commission, the Los Angeles Department of
Cultural Affairs and the National Endowment for the Arts partially support
Red Hen Press.
First Edition

Published by Red Hen Press
Pasadena, CA
www.redhen.org

for Alexi, Zoe, Maya

CONTENTS

The Building   11
Icepicks on 93rd Street   13
The Boys Who Climb the Marble Squares
    on the Soldiers and Sailors Monument   15
Marbles   17
Stickball on 88th Street   21
Lucy Thibodeau   24
A Bloody Saturday Night   27
Leah Scott   30
Sammy Propp   32
Donald Franklyn Pierce   34
Dreaming   36
Blondie   37
Snow in the Gully   39
Skating   41
Overnight Train   44
The Woods   47
Street People   49
Women   52
The Family   57
How the Doorman Lets My Father Come
    Upstairs Unseen Through a Side Entrance   59
The Couch   61
Neil the Elevatorman   64
Mother   66
Bessie   71
Howard   73
Beatrice   77

Subway   79
Diving   81
White Nights   84
The Bible   86
Quakers   88
Shirley   91
Selling   94
The Call   99

STICKBALL ON 88th STREET

THE BUILDING

Babe Ruth lives on the other
side of the court. His brother-in-law
    jumped from the 18th
    story into the handball
area where we play until tenants
get angry. I heard the thump
    when I was in
    bed. The Babe gave
me a baseball diploma. The same
elevator man Joe who slapped me
    for not being nice
    to Jerry (wasn't true)
took me to the Babe's for
the photo that came out in
    The Mirror. Sunday afternoons
    we hear Father Coughlin
and Hitler live, shrieking on the
radio. Everyone hates Hitler. When there's
    a strike, new men
    keep billy clubs by
the doors. I like the scabs
as much as Ruddy and Joe
    outside to whom we
    bring sandwiches. I heard
Ruddy got hit trying to bust
in. They almost broke his head.
    It's funny for men
    to ride me up

the elevator. I always run downstairs.
They slow me down as I
    race for the outside
    into the North Pole
wind and the gully. But often
I spend the afternoon in
    a corner of the
    elevator, going up and
down in the tired coffin.
When no one else is riding,
they let me close the brass
    gate. I do it
    like a grownup stiff.

ICEPICKS ON 93ʳᵈ STREET

I am wandering like a sailor
on the Drive. Eliot told me
    Life had an article
    on how babies are
born, with pictures of women.
I don't suppose I'll see *Life*,
    but oh it's great
    to think about them
slowly. Women. Between their legs is
what I see. Suddenly three icepicks
    are against my ribs.
    It's the Price gang.
Brothers. They've been to a reformatory,
I have a nickel but jam
    it into the lining
    and when they search
me they get nothing. But I'm
like stone, unbreathing, so scared I
    feel like a pickle
    with their spikes inside.
When the Price gang is gone
all those blond heads and pug
    noses seem alike. The
    Irish toughs from Amsterdam!
I don't hate them. I thought
they'd be worse. *Empty your pockets*
    or we'll stick you.
    I didn't think they

would. But I can't walk there
for weeks, as if the brothers
    are always there, waiting
    to knife me for
cash. Eliot said the girls uptown let
you touch their hair or get
    in their bed if
    you have money. Now
I'm cocky. I've been held up
with icepicks against a dark wall.
    Maybe like the sailors
    I'll kiss a girl.

THE BOYS WHO CLIMB THE MARBLE SQUARES ON THE SOLDIERS AND SAILORS MONUMENT

Last year one of them got
killed. He fell from the marble
    cylinder into the pocket
    between the columns and
onto the tar. Most of those
kids are colored. I got up
    twice to the eagle.
    It is just three
stories to the bird, easy climb,
but it took weeks to get
    myself to do it,
    and I stay there
all afternoon, enjoying my warm nest,
terrified to look down. The boys
    who climb the marble
    squares just hop into
my booth and shimmy to the
ledge under the squares. They always
    run around it first,
    shouting dirty words. Then
the real climb. The ones who
look poorest in their undershirts are
    the toughest. They crawl
    up, insects. Very few

make the rim circling round near
the ceiling. Then no place to
    go but to hang
    a while from it,
dangle as from a far wing,
hang all their toughness over the
    ocean of air that
    won't hold them up

MARBLES

During the marble season we control
89th Street. Cars edge by. Only
    cabs use their horns.
    Alfred is a big
winner. He's got cigar boxes loaded
with peewees and fat aggies he
    keeps in a schoolbag
    like a banker. I
am sloppier and have never gone
into the business of setting boxes
    out in the gutter
    for guys to shoot
at the square holes. I hang
a few leather pouches from my
    belt and the rest
    are crunched in pockets
so I can hardly sit at school.
I make lots of noise when
    I run. The art
    of shooting from midway
in the street at a single,
between a double, or through a
    hole is not luck.
    It takes good eyes
and thought. Of course you have
to hit boxes that pay off.
    I'm a shooter, and
    do okay if the

street isn't warped, but I'm not
an acer. Some guys hit all
    the time or flip
    you for baseball cards
and clean you out. We've trouble
when a car wants to park
    and the doorman makes
    us move. Then Alfred
and I sometimes go to his
house where we drop marbles on
    passing cars from the
    roof. We can hear
Jan Pierce rehearsing by holding an
ear against the elevator shaft door.
    I like to jump from
the indoor balcony down
to the sofa, and don't really
know why it upsets Mrs. Freedman
    so much. I always
    like to jump or
climb. When I leave Alfred, I
go back to the street where
    it's getting dark. A
    big skinny red-haired kid
is walking by himself. And suddenly
I wrestle him to the ground—
    I don't know why
    I start it. We

roll on the sidewalk a while
and then I get back to
        the marbles where there
        are only a few
boxes still going. It's cold and
the Park wind rips through blue
        light and smashes me,
        gets through my knickers
as I head for the Drive.
I don't use the entrance but
        turn the wild corner,
        climb up the square
limestone facing to my bedroom window
and like a thief slip inside.

STICKBALL ON 88th STREET

I'm not much good at stickball
and the kids are tough. Somehow
    it's my turn. In
    comes the rubber ball
slowly in a dream like a
planet that won't spin. It comes
    close, a blazing milky
    rubber pea. I swing.
Bop! My childhood skids along windows,
dropping fair behind a manhole. I
    race scared, ripping out
    to second, miles away.
I must tag the lamp post first,
get by the toughs, not piss
    in my pants or
    bite my tongue. Why
didn't I dump the marbles when
I got up to bat? They
    rattle in my knickers
    pockets. Second is far
as Maiden Lane. If I slip
I'm out! No one's my friend
    on this block, If
    I make it, I'll
pass semaphore and learn to kip
on the highbar. The boys are
    screaming for me to
    run. For me! I

Round second. Two kids are yelling
up the street, after the ball,
        as it bounces toward
        mad yellow taxis thumping
down West End. I fly home
through the mobs of black angels.
        Tonight I'll even snatch
        supper from the dog.
The ball floats home. I'm safely
standing on the side with guys
        shoving me, beating on
        me with their fists.
Good job, you punk. You're fuckin'
Joe DiMaggio. They won't stop pounding
        me and I'll never
        get to bat again.

Lucy Thibodeau

My first memory of life is
you holding me on steps outside
    a hospital where they
    snipped out my tonsils.
Maybe I am two. We are
already engaged and go steady till
    I am five. Overhead,
    a NY cement sky
more like a photo than a
memory. I am so in love
    with you! Mother is
    jealous and you won't
let her come near. When you
marry the doorman Jimmy and leave
    and have your own
    child (who never learns
to walk), I feel bleak. All
I know for sure is how
    good when Jimmy dumps
    you (I am nine)
and we fix it for me
to come daily to your place
    for lunch between classes.
    I run up the
tenement stairs to the smell of
soup. I kiss a French beauty
    and we talk like
    old times. Now the

adventure will last for life (I
think) and never see you again.
    In the fall my
    sister writes that you
have aged, are thin, are spirited
as always. I think of you
    only a few times
    a year. You formed
me perhaps and time unformed the
work. When you kissed me, what
    did you think? Were
    mountains infinitely tall? Was
the day just one soup
of 10,000 splendid vermicelli soups
    for the elegant court
    of our futurity? Did
you know you would ever get
skinny and die? Other women I
    have loved disappeared too.
    They form you. You
touch them and go away. You
held me for five years, Lucy.
    What luck to have
    known you, a beauty,
and then you fled for 100
years into the snow to live
    in poverty with your
    sisters. We come, we

go. It is not different from
death. Thanks for coming to
     the window each noon
     to look for me
down the stairwell, for not fooling
yourself about how we had to
     fail, about how good
     we were, how like
insects, cities, and firmaments, we appear
and flare and fall apart. In
     that Maine village with
     your wheelchair son, I
am outside the house on the
Auburn hill, looking in, completely dumb.

A BLOODY SATURDAY NIGHT

I had been boxing for years.
Now at eleven, skinny but good
    muscles, I am the
    only one who dares
fight Lenny. Lenny is an animal,
my friend, but he demolishes anyone
    who spars with him.
    So I can't believe
that I'm really up to Lenny.
But my buddies do and I
    am starting to think
    I have a chance
of putting him away. That photo
at Old Orchard Beach still haunts
    me. There I am
    against a wall, my
legs twined to keep it in.
And the second picture with my
    pants all wet, still
    smiling. It is now
the joke in our house. And
this pisher—who used to have
    to hang camp sheets out
    to sun-dry in front
of anyone who cares to look
and laugh — is taking on Lenny
    in front of mobs
    of campers. I'm David

facing a monstrous Philistine in the
same hall where during morning service
    they told the story
    of the dancer between
two armies, more glorious than Pharaoh
in an ivory chariot. The bell
    brings us out. Lenny
    has lightning-quick mitts. We
dance around the huge ring, trading
jabs. I smash him in the
    bread-basket. The ref
    warns me. I tag
him behind the ear. He gets
his glove in my armpit, and
    we waddle like pros.
    I hear nothing. As
I move in I make an
old mistake: Lenny pops me under
    the chin just when
    my tongue is out.
A stream of blood jets eight
feet in a red arc from
    my mouth, and suddenly
    the ref saves Lenny
on the run, from a holocaust.
They take me from the hall
    to a nurse who
    stitches up my tongue.

It is dark. Though my career
fizzled, the sand by the lake
    and ping-pong tables holds
    me up in glory.

LEAH SCOTT

I always have good friends. But
when I leave them for supper,
    I talk to Leah
    who is cooking or
still scrubbing. She lets me sit
on her back while she washes
    the kitchen floor. Leah
    doesn't talk much except
on nights she sleeps over. She's
in my brother's bed, and screams
    Get down, Satan in
    her sleep. I never
heard her yell before. She was
the only black woman at Mother's
    funeral. I overheard someone
    say Mother had to
get *schwarze* maids so father would
leave them alone. Leah's a good
    woman and I love
    her a lot. When
she doesn't stay over I am
lonely, which is the real me.
    My window faces Jersey,
    a dark place except
for a few neon signs
and the Bridge. Jersey's lonely too.
    I watch the shore
    for hours. The Crisco

light and—each 60 seconds—the
time. I wait hours and weeks
    for signs to change
    their words, hoping for
at least one word to change
everything I know. I could wait
    like a man sitting
    on a black horse
in a garden of gigantic flowers.
Years would be easy to wait.
    Some nights I stare
    until Leah comes in
at 6:30. She has the milk,
the subway paper. I hug her
    just once, gulp breakfast,
    and hunt for friends.

SAMMY PROPP

I don't know whether Sammy Propp
is smart, wise, or dumb like
    Jerry who goes to
    school though something's wrong.
But Sammy knows things. He knows
Hebrew. He has a big smile
    like a half-opened book
    and his black hair is
short like a bureau brush. And
what feet! His black shoes don't
    end. They stick out
    under chairs, on rugs.
We play punch-ball and Sammy comes
along when we sled the gully.
    He's the extra. Alfred
    says he knows other
languages. Whenever I go to his
apartment, I wait in a hall
    with benches and books
    and ten grandfathers who
keep their hats on and don't
see us. The furniture is black.
    Alfred says Sammy is
    religious but he's so
nice, it is hard to believe.
On Saturday morning when we don't
    have school and take
    off for the river,

Sammy's got a big hat on
in a room with old men.
    Sundays we often hike
    somewhere together. He smiles
and I think he may be
smart, but I don't understand him. We're
    friends. Until Alfred said
    it, I never saw
how short Sammy is! He walks
with enormous steps in Temple trousers,
    always talking to me,
    smiling, asking me things.
Eliot, who loves to dress up
in fancy old Irish hunting garb,
    says Sammy studies Talmud.
    What's that? I wonder.
We're all the same age, but
Sammy's voice is deep as if
    he got a cello
    stuck in his throat.

DONALD FRANKLYN PIERCE

What a good winter! Mr. Leopold
and Frank are with me. Frank's
    living in the house
    and Mr. Leopold comes
almost every second night to play
pinochle. Three men! Frank is 25,
    Leopold 60, I'm 10.
    Waldo Leopold lives at
the Hotel Paris. He wears white
suits, polka dot handkerchiefs and bowties
    so we won't spot
    his sparkly bald platter
but it still shines like his smile
when he demonstrates a corny trick.
    Frank works for Oscar,
    my brother-in-law. He's in
law school, smokes a pipe as
a handsome actor plays an ensign.
    He kids me in
    sporty ways that are
genteel and like Bowdoin in Maine
where his great-great grandfather went to
    school (with Hawthorne and
    Longfellow) before he became
President. This winter I am crazy
about Mr. Leopold and Frank. They
    also teach me poker
    and we gamble sums

which are worth so many marbles
my cigar boxes could not hold
    them. When we gamble
    I can stay up
into grownup hours, but when Frank
chases me off to bed, he makes
    me feel like Peewee
    Reese getting power sleep
before slamming hits against the Giants.
Waldo lets me puff his cigar.
    Often at supper, Frank
    and I go on
long walks down to Riverside Park
along the third rail, the Hudson
    where sewage floats out.
    He talks to me
of women and other adult matters.
My parents are vaguely away down
    south, and I am
    suddenly with tremendous friends.
After Frank leaves, there are no
more poker games or danger walks
    into the night park.
    He's drafted into the
Army and is killed in France.
All gone are our winter and
    my pals. Poor Frank
    will not be President.

DREAMING

I search the sky. The window
facing the Hudson and Jersey coast
    is my Saracen tower
    from where I spot
bonfires of Crusaders, or blue cops
clubbing the park trees methodically as
    they walk their beat.
    At twilight I study
God whom I've been making up
since I remember. He is not
    like my father, who
    is good. God is
what they say father is: an
angry, crazy man. So I've abolished
    God, because I want
    my Dad. I see
a white horse at night over
an iceland with hungry leopard seals.
    Suddenly the new moon
    is frozen like a dancer.

BLONDIE

Mother is calm like our Chinese
rug—and firm like the Tree
    of Life a painter
    put in the wool.
Her eyes are Maine forest green.
She is real as a painting
    and just as constant.
    Dad calls her Blondie
and she's unreal as an angel
because she keeps mountains of heaven
    inside her, which I
    know nothing of, and
only Sunday morning when I invade
Mom and Dad's room and bounce
    on their bed do
    I rouse her to
shoo me off like a monkey
out of India. But she never
    screams or weeps or
    bellyaches. I listen to
the Green Hornet or read funnies
till supper when she can't get
    me to eat onions.
    She doesn't talk easily
but her word is a temple.
She is good, and never gives
    me hell, yet her
    word is there, unsaid

and strong. It's strange to be
so strong and soft at once:
    a woman. She is
    a mystery to me
like women or God or solid
geometry which I'll know one day
    in high school. She
    likes me I know
because of what I overhear her
say to Blanche or Sadie or
    other friends. Mother is
    clear and deep like
a Chinese print with mist, and
I love her like some cloud
    beyond quiet bamboo mountains
    (far inside the frame).

SNOW IN THE GULLY

Before they wrecked the gully by
putting in a City Park playground
    (I admit with good
    punch-ball games and highbars),
we can sled all the way
down to the tracks. When winter
    comes, the gale off
    the Hudson kicks you
freezing back up the wind-tunnel street.
We grab our sleds and grease
    the rails with butter.
    Then drag them through
the iron wind. I share mine
with Eliot or Sammy. Since Eliot's
    fat, I'm on top
    and he steers. Sammy
goes down alone. A million kids
on the slope, screaming! I bellyflop
    down, trying to glide
    far enough to make
the third rail. Then the climb
through the sky of iceballs hurled
    at us from kids
    on top. Eliot hops
on me, squashing the slush through
my shirt. Both of us steer.
    It's as if we're
    dropping down sheer ice,

going like hell until we smash
into a big tree. The sled's
    okay but my wrist
    is cut. I slog
home through the black air. Cars
are groping brightly along the Drive
    toward food and warmth.
    Mother makes me drip
off in the hall. My head's
still frozen. Sammy's got lost. But
    tomorrow we'll double up
    so he can steer.

SKATING

As a scout I'm a loser
and slob. I make First Class
    but how? In the
    New Jersey forest where
we bivouac, I cook a pie
by filling pre-made dough with canned
    stewed tomatoes. I lay
    the leaky mess in
an outdoor fire with potatoes, and
when it burns black, I take
    it to the scoutmaster.
    You eat, you pass.
So I pass cooking. I also
win an axe for selling raffles,
    but my uniform never
    fits. I'd rather skate
than march. When spring gets rid
of the ice, the boys start
    hockey. I'm not good
    enough for the team
and skate off, gliding lengths
from the street to street. I've gone all
    the way to Harlem
    and the East Side.
No place lies beyond my rollers.
I dance backwards and take leaps
    like an artist. And
    I like to go

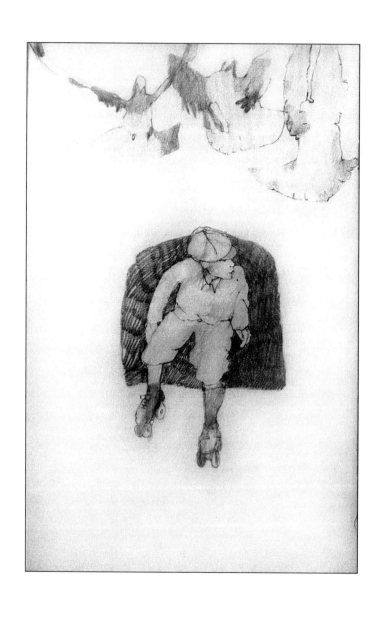

alone. I find my skinny body
as it flies through the wind.
 On Sunday when I
 gaze out the window
at the warships sailoring the
river, and my head is bursting
 in this empty house,
 I take my skates
to the Drive. I put them
on as an actor puts on
 paint. Then I skirt
the flocks of families and pigeons;
race from tier to tier of
 marble sky, & roll across
 stone benches in exultation!

Overnight Train

We go to camp by Pullman
from Grand Central Station. 50 groups
    leave the madhouse
    Sunday. I try to
nap in the luggage hammock, then
go constantly up and down from
    my berth into
    the washroom, which stinks
of steam and smoke, whose cold
and hot faucets are curved like
    the dining car's oversize
    spoons. Amid the clacking
metals, the black porter is bent
asleep. Back in the starched sheets
    and tight tan blanket,
    I hear the wheels
all night, the squeaking, the ponderous
thumping and whizz. As we speed
    I gaze eagerly at
    the darkness. I am
the night. The black firmament starts
on my sheet and goes outward
    to planets on the
    ceiling 500 miles away.
I draw open the heavy curtain
and watch cows looking at me,
    see white clapboard sheds
    as upright as gravestones.

My eye is huge and tingles,
holding all those outdoor ghosts and
    half moon. Finally, sleep
    lies on me. I
watch it come, control it like
the narrow berth-lamp over the window.
    Each time I turn
    the bulb on, all
becomes a small cell with fire.
I got into sleep, deep into
    a time absolutely still
    except for the wheels
alertly blazing North. When tiny morning
tapes the fields with amazing sun,
    I hear cocks, bells.
    The cows are still
giving the yellow meadows a haircut.
I shimmy down & rock toward breakfast.

The Woods

There is a trail around the lake
in the woods that goes up
    to a mountain. We
    hike in the morning.
Hal picks up wintergreen and chews
the leaf. I have a canteen
    and a Bowie knife.
    We are looking for
the secret meadow where the blueberries
are already out. I fall behind
    (I always do, even
    later on the Great
Wall) and get lost. *We'll meet
on the mountain* someone yells. In
    northern Maine the air
    is knifeblade cool in
July, Caesar's month, and the pines
don't know ice from summer. But
    I come on an orchard with barbed wire
and poison ivy on the rails.
Abandoned. The apples are pieces of
    red fire and taste
    like fire water. I
have to shit. I'll catch up.
Am worried about the leaves mixed
    with dirt I have
    to use. Voices fade.
Under an apple tree is a perfect

stick for whittling a walking cane.
    I sit in the
    sun and pare bark
from the cedar branch. It's nice
in the sun, lying down. Sun
    floats up there, a
    ship, and directly under
it is me. I close my
eyes and it is violet under
    the lids, a sea
    almost. For a few
hours I sleep. Then get up
and finish the cane. When I
    get to the mountain,
    no one's there, but
I collect blueberries, all I can
cart back. The sun is gone
    as I turn back.
    I hear remote voices,
Billy! Where are you? Night tastes
good. No wind. No yapping birds
    but the owls boohoo.
    I bound quickly through
the woods, stumbling against a birch,
squashing the berries in my pocket.
    Some hours after midnight
    I find my tent.

STREET PEOPLE

Old people sit on benches next
to the subway on upper Broadway
    or along the Drive.
    At times they talk,
often they put their hands flat
on the arm-rests and gaze for
    hours. They seem to
be thinking but their bodies are
not moving. Some are what are
    called refugees. Near Grant's
    Tomb with its lively
stone horse, there's always one old
lady whose face is shaped like
    a Singer sewing machine,
    whose hair is white
grass, who uses her cane to
knock nuts across the octagonal paving
    stones on which both
    squirrels and pigeons circle
her. On a sidestreet I see
a man in sandwich boards advertising
    sneakers pull his penis
    out and leak next
to the gutter. He has white
stubble on his cheek, fat shoes
    and looks blank when
    I look at him.
I am curiously ashamed. His eyes

scan the buildings, then look down
  as he clears his
  nose. Up by Joan
of Arc, and old guy, round
as a tomato, in a narrow
  store sells pastrami sandwiches
  to us between classes
at 4¢ apiece. *Who next!*
who nex! he shouts. I hardly
  recall my mother's mother
  and father. She outlived
him, though her hands were shaking
and we couldn't make the slightest
  noise. When the ambulance
  came last night, its
white body sucked in a stretcher
and the machine sped off. The
  doorman said the super's
  girl died of polio.
I wonder what I'd do if
swimming across Lake Beebee my arms
  tired, if I took
  in sky water, drowned
and faded to the bottom and became
the whole world in my head
  and couldn't get back
  in time for classes.

WOMEN

Eliot says babies come out of
a woman's stomach through
    her legs. He tells
    me so one afternoon
as we walk by the river
at nightfall. I've never seen where
    a girl pisses from
    and think no one
has. If I were a girl
for a few days, I'd look
    with a mirror and
    find out every secret.
I don't know any girls. They
play jacks and hopscotch, prance around
    on the sidewalk while
    we're in the street.
About five years ago when I
was six—so long ago it's
    hazy—I saw, or
    almost saw, two girls
behind some rocks in the park
pull off their panties on purpose.
    They were kids, too,
    jumping up and down
and yelling. I knew two women
for a short time. Last year
    I walked Sarah Whitehall
    home, and even went

up to her apartment and met
her mother. I liked her. It was
    odd and fun walking
    on the sidewalk with a girl. We
talked about Joe Louis who had
    just put Max Schmeling
    in the hospital. Sarah
asked me to a party where they
would play spin-the-bottle, post office, and
    strip poker. I went
    but she'd moved away
and all we did was dunk
for apples and play blind-man's-bluff.
    Varda Karni is different,
    She's dark. Her hair
is beautiful. Her parents take her
to many cities in the Middle
    East. I'm good at
    school and tell her
what I know about astronomy and
art. I have a crush. She
    seems to fly in
    from far Fifth Avenue
and Ethical Culture. She has swept
through the Museum of Natural History
    and smiles at me.
    I don't know what
she thinks. A mystery. I give

her a copy of Homer's *Odyssey*
    and one day at
    the door she comes
to bring a big letter and quickly
goes. I take it to the blue
    living room, open two
    sheets of white paper
inside each other, and a third
sheet carefully folded to a small
    square. It is blank
    inside. Not a word,
not even Varda. Eliot says he
knows a lot more about women,
    as we slog home,
    & one day will tell.

THE FAMILY

Sometimes I go down to Wall Street
and the office on Maiden Lane.
    We come up out
    of the subway like
birds soaring out of a sewer.
Goldsmiths, Pildes! These stores are cities
    with everything man invented
    in crystal and steel
like Brahms played by Mrs. Friedburg
my teacher from Germany. Dad is
    walking with me. NY
    spring sun makes us
feel happy. Suddenly Dad takes off
his felt hat with a curse.
    A pigeon on
    its light gray dome.
Till then I didn't know birds
could do that to people. Before
    we go into Schrafts,
    I race ahead to
a lamp post and climb up. He
doesn't mind. I remember they found
    the felt hat on
    the roof when he
jumped into the spring sky. Smell
of mint and blueberry twinges in
    the air. We're eating
    cheese pie. The waitresses

are fat and creamy like the
pie. Up in the office Dad
     lends cash to a
     black Jewish sailor who
missed his ship. Mom, Dad, and
I subway home with three newspapers.
     Tired. Dad alertly reads
     The World Telegram. Tonight
we'll all hear *Information Please.* By
morning when I hear father screaming,
     You God damn bitch,
     you. You God damn
bitch, you. He is furious and
gets out the door. Mother and
     I go back into
     the rooms. As when
the bird shat on the light
gray dome of Dad's new hat,
     I'm surprised. I feel
     thin and now alone.

How the Doorman
Lets My Father Come
Upstairs Unseen Through
a Side Entrance

At twilight the doorman and I
go around the corner to a
    door I never saw
    that lets my father
in directly to the back stairs.
The cars on the Drive are
    sedate, carrying authority from
    downtown, uptown. We are
New Yorkers and don't own one.
Where is my father coming from?
    A place they have
    cars? From the city?
It's the first time he's here,
and no reason for neighbors, who
    are strangers, to know.
    He is not afraid
but is not beaming. It's funny
to sneak him in like Jews
    out of a ghetto
    to get food, as
if he were guilty for being
my mother's husband. He is happy
    we make it in,
    as if we went
out on the road and sold

a diamond. I'm up again when
    he goes down white
    iron back steps, by
the boiler room, and up to the
wood-and-brass sidedoor. There are only one
    or two solitary cars
    rolling outside. It is
almost twilight. I kiss my father
before we open the door. He
    steps unshaven into half
    light. Maybe in a
week he'll call from out there,
from miles into the light, and
    we'll meet at the
    zoo or down below.

THE COUCH

Since dad split, we moved from
the windy Drive to two big rooms
    on Central Park South,
    snooty but no kids.
When Aunt Jane or someone else
stays over, I sleep by myself
    (the guest's with Mother)
    on the living room couch.
The big room has a blue
Persian rug, a Bubble boy done in
    1900 by Mrs. Adams
    our neighbor in Maine,
and fake marble antiques from France
of the 17th century done in
    1810. When I perform
    acrobatics on the rug
I stop and look at the
Bubbleboy looking at me. His hair
    is angel gold. He
    never finishes the pipe.
I think he's me. Tonight I stay up.
No one tells me about my
    body except to eat
    quickly, although I'm deeply
curious. In the bathtub my dong
floats and I steer it through
    sponges and soap foam
    until the last water

drains out and its face lies
on the cold porcelain. Now I'm
    on my back. NY
    stars and the lights
from the Zoo come in through
the Venetian blinds, in the dark
    livingroom. I am playing
    acrobatics with my dong,
playing pinochle quickly. It's a Jack
of Spades looking for a Queen
    of Hearts. I seize
    and hurt it! It's
climbing up away from me when
it shudders and shoots out something
    not piss, the sweetest
    pain on the planet.
It drains me and the fury
suddenly stops. I think I've leaked
    or broken a piece
    of my body. I'm
alarmed and happy. Maybe it's ok.
I say nothing. Late next evening
    I can hardly wait
    till the next room
is silent. The Bubbleboy is dark
and only those bits of light
    from the city sky
    shine over the couch

where I try out the secret
game again. With slow fury I
    play the same Jack
    until I get lost
eagerly in a flooding white sea.
It comes! It goes out almost
    as strong. The Queen.
    I'm in 100 rooms.

Neil the Elevatorman

Neil's teeth are rotted, his hair
blond and stringy but his eyes
    are weak sea blue
    and kind. When his
car is not busy he lets
me ride up and down. At
    times he comes to
    the door to talk.
He is a vegetarian. We had
a maid named Meek Shyness who
    belonged to Father Divine
    but Neil's the first
vegetarian. He is the first intellectual
I met (what they call him
    in our house with a laugh).
    They are suspicious of
Neil, though they say he is
kind and probably harmless. He's poor,
    lives alone and reads
    all the time. I
am one of his real friends,
he tells me, and for me
    he is very important.
    The afternoon the Normandie
was burning, he took me up
to the roof and we stood
    with crowds of people
    watching the flames. It

was the first time so many
people from the building were together
    talking easily. Neil gives
    me books to read
and I take food from the icebox
for him. I am surprised and
    happy that he has
    different thoughts on everything.
I want to be like him,
to be poor, live in one
    room, eat what I
    will, and be alone
to think differently. He doesn't care
what they call him. I overhear
    he's been let go
    for talking to tenants.

MOTHER

Mother has natural gold hair, green
    eyes, a cameo face.
    The hairdo is Greek
and the flesh a slab of
blue-gold marble cut from Mt. Penteli.
    She and sister Jane,
    who is dark, were
the beauties of Lewiston and Auburn,
though like Chinese in European Shanghai
    they were not allowed
    to be at a
public dance. She worships her father
and cares for Uncle Bert the
    Seventh Day Adventist, but
    never forgave her sister
Eva's apostate marriage to him. Since
father has been away from home
    most of the time,
    my older sister married,
and Howard in the Navy, we
sleep in twin beds in one
    of our big rooms
    overlooking the Park Zoo,
She's a good dancer and fun
to see Garbo movies with. We
    watch Chico tapping ivory
    on the Roxy stage.
When I head for the Paramount—

three big Saturday shows—she's got
    the bagged lunch ready.
    Although her talk is
chaste and spare (she's quite shy),
in her way she is profound
    like Praxilla who left
    only a few fragments
about pears and the moon. Meals
are her exercise in speed eating
    and a test of how
    much fire coffee keeps
before it's gulped whole like Jonah.
After we've eaten like Barbary pirates,
    I do the dishes
    and she never lets
me get down to homework without
my scrubbing every micro-germ into
    Babo death. She takes
    her bath very late
and leaves the door ajar for
the steam. I often try to
    look, but the mirror
    is at the wrong angle
except for a flash when she
steps out. We don't talk about
    father, but one afternoon
    she told Aunt Jane
(I couldn't help hearing it) that

I loved him more than her
and didn't care what
he did. I feel
awful, because I do love Dad
and love to be with him
and hear his stories,
always daring and true,
and he likes Rembrandt and wants
me to be something like that
Dutchman who paints dark
beggars in noble clothes.
Why does she care? I admire
her just as much. To be
fair, she tells only
Aunt Jane, not me
but I know she disapproves. When
word comes of his death leap,
she's weeping and is
outraged: Why did he
pull that stunt? Why? Mother
is not religious. She never spoke
about God (and Christ
is a fearful word
because so many of us were
killed in the good rabbi's name),
yet she always lights
a glass with a
candle for her father each year

after his death. Her father is
     her man. She keeps
     his picture by the
memory glass: handsomely bearded. She often
comments on his perfect silver hair,
     all of it there,
     unlike Dad's. I am
preparing to go away, to a
Quaker School that's good like her.
     She almost never complains
     except the day she
becomes sixty. I show my friends
a picture of her, proving her
     figure and face are
     lovely like legend.
She has lots of pain
when the taxi takes us through
     the Park to Mount
     Sinai Hospital. It
is June. As the cab winds,
she tells us this is her
     last time to see
     the Park. Mother never
talks much. Her words are soft,
brave as a legend. She will
     lie down under knives
     and not breathe honey
of Hymettos near her marble hill,

but suck poisonous fumes and not
    breathe again. What can
    I say? She knows.

BESSIE

Cousin Bessie is a red. She
is our only political and poor
  relation. We all like
  Bessie and say she's
a good woman whatever she thinks.
She came from Russia with nothing
  but a pair of
  black galoshes. Dad likes
to take her on when she
comes for Thursday supper (Leah's off)
  and always gets cold
  meals, maybe a pineapple
upside-down cake, if any is left.
We sit down to borscht, horseradish
  and gefilte fish. Bessie
  dumped her husband Max
who fought with the Lincoln Brigade
and lost a finger. *How's Max?*
  I ask her one
  night. That bum? she
answers. Max studied watchmaking but refused
to eat on anything but newspapers.
  Bessie used to live
  in a Bronx basement
in which the icebox leaked, but
she's downtown now and her feet
  don't hurt so much
  from walking. Bess brims

with love. She loves Stalin and really cares
for workers and all poor people.
    Her kisses are famous:
    huge, noisy and slubbery,
and she's so kind and concerned.
She always asks first about me,
    Billy. I go to
    see her and we
talk politics—my first lessons—but
she warns me not to repeat
    all this to my
    parents. She's always worked,
worked. Recently she took a few trips
and came back hatted and smiling.
    We are her only
    relations. Her age is
a mystery and joke at home.
She hasn't called so we go
    downtown. Bessie's on the
    floor, a week dead.

HOWARD

An older brother beats you up,
slams you with a wooden bedpost
    and chokes you to
    the floor. You fight
every day. A battle of pounds.
I was in the Maine mansion
    when he came running
    into the house crying,
bleeding from the mouth. A girl
jumped off the pipe of a
    home-made seesaw and he
    broke his front tooth.
I broke my tooth in the gully,
playing football, when a guy fell
    on me and I
    hit a rock as
I tried to nail the pass.
Howard took me iceskating on 92nd
    on the tennis courts.
    He goes out sailing
with his buddies. On my first
time around my ankles are weak.
    I fall and someone
    skates over my finger
but the person never knew it.
At home he is the one
    who knows almost everything.
    He brought us Wimpy,

a mutt who stole my lambchop
out of my plate and ran
    under the couch. I
    got under the couch
to grab it back and it bit
my hand. He dresses up and
    has smart friends like
    Richard who wears glasses.
Howard's a sissy to wear such
fine clothes. Often he takes Mother
    out. They water-ski, eat
    in nice restaurants. He
doesn't see father much. I guess
they hate each other, yet then
    they don't. Mainly they're
    both away. My brother
is an artist and a snob.
He is a brain. He knows
    what he wants to
    do, and cannot fail.
I think of him in navy suits,
elegant ties, in rooms perfectly built
    like a black refrigerator,
    saints on the wall,
and he is the artist who
made them. I know he wants
    to shape me too
    (too much for me)

and when no one knows what
to do for me, he cares
        wisely and sends me
        to live with Quakers.

BEATRICE

Who is my sister? I used to
dream of her—a photo on
    the dresser, an actress
    in high school. She's
like mother, really from the North,
not just born there like me.
    Once in our house
    on the steep hill
in Auburn, the Victorian villa under
the chestnut trees, I wander through
    the halls and rooms
    with shining brass bedposts
where the Chinese merchant, the butcher
and tailor each has a room.
    Beyond the den, in
    a series of almost
endless chambers, is a bathroom where,
I heard, my sister is taking
    a bath. I wander
    innocently, playing the child,
till I'm at the ultimate door
in the maze, and by mistake
    open it. My sister
    is full of soap,
half out of the water and
facing me. She yells while I
    slam it and race
    down the corridor with

people after me! When I was
at summer camp I used to
      daydream again and again
      of getting left behind
in the washhouse where the women
came Thursday afternoons to take showers
      after the lake. I'd
      stand on a toilet
and see maybe ten big women
and not be caught. Beatrice is
      twelve years older and
      has boyfriends who take
me in the rumbleseat for rides.
The one she loves later goes
      to war and dies.
      My sister is very
nimble with words. She laughs like
a star of Edward Little High School.
      Beatrice is the first
      woman beauty I know.

Subway

The subway goes everywhere in the
known world. It drones into Pakistan
    and its Polo Grounds,
    to the Wailing Wall
of ancient Jerusalem, to Spain and
China, and the old Dutch colony
    of Harlem. It squeaks
    around African heights, and
when it snows, we wait on
the platform in the barren frost
    like Eskimos. I doze
    behind the papers. ITALIAN
GIRL BORN WITH 12 TEETH, ROLLER-SKATES
AT 7 MONTHS. 5 CONS TRAPPED
    IN BASEMENT. 20,000 REDS
    KILLED BY FINN SKIERS.
Suddenly a little man rushes down
the car, giving us the finger,
    with big flashing eyes,
    and shouts FUCK YOU!
to each of us separately till
he's put out. I do homework,
    English & trig. Often
    Mother sticks with me
till 14th. The cars are jammed
and serious like a church when

            the evening IRT Express
            takes Wall Street home.
When I go home from downtown
with Dad, there's such a roar
            we can't talk, so
            I read or sleep
against his shoulder. The black trains
rumble to every port in Hades.
            We seldom come up
            for air except in
Brooklyn, when we are suddenly
            miles over the street and stores.
            Once I saw a
            watch between the rails,
hopped down and grabbed it just
before the train screamed in. Now
            I take the other
            train that comes up
for air at 96th & heads West.
Sailors are sound asleep like bears
            up in luggage-racks. I'm
            a vet at trains!
For three days I sell sandwiches,
make enough to eat in dining cars
            till Idaho where Dad's
            proud I made it alone.

Diving

In Latin class I share a
seat with a boy who stinks
    of garlic and piss.
    When he talks to
me about two girls he screwed
behind a car in a Brooklyn
    parking lot, I almost
    pass out. We switched,
he tells me. *We were two
guys, and stuck 'em one*
    at a time. In the hall
    a fellow asks me if I've
heard of the new diver on
the team, *Barnstoni*, and Italian kid.
    They wrote up our
    meet in the Stuyvesant
paper, misspelled my name. I practice
every afternoon at the 92nd Y.
    Once, when I was
    waiting in line to
get to the cage where they
give out locker trays, the lady
    told me I was
    a snot (though I'd
said nothing). Then through the steam
room with fat men and showers,
    and finally the pool
    with its piercing haze

of chlorine. I wear a suit,
because I dive. The others do
    laps naked—you cut
    a second off a
mile, the coach says. I place
my towel on the mosaic steps,
    stick my gum behind
    my ear, hop up
on the springboard, bounce it twice
and ease into an open pike
    one-and-a-half. After a few
    warm ups, the coach
comes over to the board. *And
keep your goddam toes pointed.* I'd
    be lost without Saul.
    He's got rimmed glasses,
is pump, his operation scar wriggles
over his towel. *And don't stick
    your tongue out when
    you take off!* On
touching bottom, I push off automatically
to the side and am up
    in no time. Once
    I came out too
soon from a two-and-a-half tuck and
slap my forehead on the water.
    I wake in the showerroom,
    my memory gone. I

don't know who I am, how
old, where I am. It takes
    a few hours to
    be okay. (I had
pushed off to the side as
in any dive, and climbed out.)
    When the team leaves,
    the lanes are free
and I practice alone. Now each
dive is a test of fear
    and form. I dance
    to the end, hurdle,
my feet driving forks into mat,
wing up over clouds, toward lamps,
    ice stars, the peak
    of aspiration, and float
forever until I break furiously in
a tuck. I seize my shins,
    spinning like a moon
    tumbling to the sea,
and open slowly, gliding a spear
into the surf. I sink deep
    to mosaic blur, bend,
    touch & begin to see.

WHITE NIGHTS

For a few days of adolescent
spring, I am so shy I
    want—walking down Broadway—
    to hide behind myself.
My eyes will break like egg —
make a mess—if a woman looks
    and I must glance
    back. Like a small
grape I gulp these stupid feelings
and late at night ponder the
    ceiling. Do I have
    a soul? Is that
a dream made up on the
toilet when there's nothing to read?
    My head is like
    a magnifying glass. Words
are big in it, and flash
through it like a loud movie.
    I lie back, trying
    to spot myself or
any face overhead. Outside a motorcycle
roars. I look inside, plunge down.
    Only light! Then lie
    for hours in dark.
Out of nervousness I pick away
the crown from my watch. I
    saw—and lost—light.
    The soul is a

thundering word with its profound O
and infinite L. I start to
    let go in whitening
    sleep. It is dawn.

THE BIBLE

After years of tutoring I go
to a school where we read
        Genesis and Samuel three
        nights a week. Miss
Fischer is excellent, the class too.
I am excited because I understand
        the text. We read
        out loud. It's for
my grandparents (who are dead) that
I am doing this, I'm told.
        They teach me to
        chant, to read black
Hebrew characters and sing according to
notation. The entire Bible becomes
        a song. Shir Hashirim,
        The Song of Songs,
is my love. I am thirteen
and therefore it is my turn
        to lead a congregation.
        The shawl is strange
but beautiful, a flag of faith
I don't have. My voice is
        small but not very
        agreeable, yet now trained
for a synagogue. One Saturday I
am taken to a butcher shop,
        and after crossing sawdust
        in the anteroom, we

are in a small unpleasant hall
with a few strangers. I go
　　to the altar and
　　chant. My training saves
me. I get through yet am
melancholy. I don't see beauty in
　　the sordid room behind
　　the butcher's. I go
on reading Ruth and the Ecclesiastes
for a full year until I spend
　　these hours with Quakers,
　　who don't read texts.

QUAKERS

My first contagion of dirty jokes,
pranks, women, peace, poems, civil rights,
    and meditation, I pick
    up at the George
School. Ethical flavor is equal to
the constant smell of breakfast cakes
    and shapes me with
    its omnipresent taste and
guilt. When Bayard Rustin comes to
sing, we slip en masse into
    a dramatic group dream
    of the Underground Railroad
when Quakers secreted the slaves North.
Now they simply want to study
    but our schoolboard won't
    let Paul Robeson's son
or any negro in—until Rustin
sings. He has opened their eyes.
    In the dorm, my
    farmer roommates keep bushels
of apples under their bunks, seeding
them among us circumspectly, as if
    measuring rainfall. Big Jack
    has an iron plate
in his skull from a tractor
crash. He claims his is eight
    inches when we measure
    our dicks in the

dark. It is raining! Buckets fall
regularly on anyone entering our trap.
        We also drop rubbers
        filled with water on
the nightwatchman—Bucketballs—as he plods
with his cane and tilting lantern.
        In the darkness boys
        sneak from room to
room. Timothy tries to get me
to jack him off. I refuse.
        I want to play kneesie
        with Betty Ross at
supper, but am shy. I have
written notes to girls hand-carried after
        lights-out. Slowly I learn,
        but never stand up
to talk when the *inner light*
comes. It has not illuminated me.
        In summer in Mexico
        we meditate at dawn
in a primitive village and read William
James aloud before our papaya breakfast.
        We boys in our
        Friends' camp are digging
privies for Indians. I am Guillermo
and fall in love with two
        college women, and will
        go everywhere to find

them. The dream begins, leading me
from lips to lips. They teach
    all kinds of love
    at the George School
(except between bodies in a bed)
and we're told not to hate or kill
    even if they are
    Nazis wiping us out.
The last love (good for life)
I don't know is mine: poems.
    Robert Frost comes to
    chant birches. While the
old man vainly entones his simple
deep verse, I hear Mr. Rustin
    singing like and angel,
    like a black nightingale.

SHIRLEY

I am thirteen and in Maine
where I was born and never
    lived. I have been
    reading Charles Dickens all
summer in the apartment we took
near Uncle Joe's. When I was
    a kid at camp,
    Maine was a lake
and the myths about Jerusalem and Job.
Now I work in a sawmill
    or watch the watchmaker
    behind his magnified eye
pick at wheels spinning in rubies,
which might be huge gold steam engines
    in a dominion run
    by scorpions. Lewiston is
hot, even at night. I meet
my cousin Shirley. She is tall,
    skinny and to me
    beautiful. She is spiritual:
a woman and a ghost who
comes to talk about the Russians
    and the English novelists,
    about us or life.
She is on a Victorian couch,
I'm in a wicker chair.
    Our words are easy
    and deep. Only we

say them for the first time
in our century. Is this me?
    She is a surprise.
    Though I never knew,
now it is natural to feel
fire and get up and go
    to the couch and
    for us to hug
long, with understanding. I don't remember
if our lips touch, but that
    first (and last) day
    we're far beyond words.

SELLING

Father has lost everything: the business,
his wife and children, his wild
    confidence. I'm with him
    for a long summer at
the Greystone Hotel. I have to
study Latin and when we're not
    talking or out selling,
    I follow Julius Caesar
into Gallia and that farthest outpost
where the hairy Britons live. Our
    room faces Broadway, but
    we're high enough not
to hear the noise. The Greystone
has known better days. We say
    we don't care. It's
    good to be together.
He shows me how to shave
and I practice carefully, imitating his
    stroke and the way
    he uses his fingers.
He has nothing left from the
company but three valises: mainly straps,
    eight fancy gold watches
    in modern shapes, some
semiprecious stones and a few
small diamonds. We figure about $500.
    Enough to live through
    the summer. And then?

What we sell we share for
rent and food. I am thrilled
    because I am with
    dad. He's showing me
things, and we often chat through
the night, from bed to bed,
    with the deepest confidence.
    I adore him, and
he always tells me I'm his
one love. But he is pained
    and depressed, though he says
    with me he's not.
We take the IRT to Wall
Street and systematically make the rounds
    of each jewelry store.
    Some of the owners,
old clients, recognize father. He gets
furious, embarrassed, or glad according to
    what they say. We
    lay the valises with
straps on the counter and dad
begins to sell. I too add
    key information about soft
    Swiss leather. If we
sell 2 gold watches and 100
watchstraps, we can make it through
    a week of diners
    and the Greystone. If

we have a good day we celebrate
at Starkers or some better place.
        Dad shows me how
        to read a newspaper
in the subway, folding it correctly.
What will we do when it's
        all gone? Yet father
        trades a few stones
and buys a diamond with all
he's got left. He sells it
        a few days later,
        doubling our cash. Now
he brings out the stones first.
On Sundays we boat or go
        out to a beach
        or watch the seals.
He's thinking of leaving the city.
We make all kinds of plans
        at night. I see
        him shaving, his face
lathered and sparkling. One late afternoon
we are strolling up Broadway. I'd been
        studying Latin words for
        hours. The top papers
on the stand read: GERMANS INVADE
POLAND! WORLD WAR! Father's going west
        and I must soon
        separate again from him

when we have finally found ways
to be free, to keep all
    riches in a tiny
    velvet cloth, and laugh.
One day in China I dream
of father coming into the room.
    He's shaving. He's come
    back to talk again.

THE CALL

I am with you in NY
at a hotel. You're in bad
    shape. Just a year
    ago in Colorado we
all walked with the wirehair bouncing
on the sidewalk. You put in
    a line direct to
    Denver and were to
civilize the world with silver goblets.
You've moved too quickly again. We
    talk about it through
    the night. You've dropped
so low I seem to be
your father now. I speak firmly,
    telling you to resist.
    Why do I speak
this way? Something prods me. Perhaps
that's what you need. But we
    do talk well. You
    know as always I
love you. And I know what
I am to you. I have
    to go back to
    Maine to finish up
the term. I don't like to
leave you. Now I'm the only
    one of us you
    see. We say goodbye

and I promise to see you
soon. Back at school, I hope
    you will pull money
    out of the sky,
you will somehow fight and feel
better. It's finals here and I'm
    cramming. My roommate Bernie
    from Austria tells me
not to worry so much. But
he's pre-med, works like hell too.
    The phone rings. Dad.
    Can you come down
right away to NY? "You must
be crazy," I say, "This is
    exam week. I'll mess
    up the whole term."
I am angry. I am surprised
that I'm impatient, but something prods
    me. Please come. "Dad,
    I can't. Please wait
a day. I'll finish finals. Are
you okay?" We talk some, but
    I can't remember words.
    He's in bad shape.
I shout at his sadness which
is piercing me. "I'll see you
    soon," I say. Click.
    I ring back to

say what train I'll take to
the city. Silence. Must be out.
        Next day he's gone.
        The week is a blur
but I'm on the golf course
with Roberto and Hans from Mexico,
        first time I've played.
        We come back late,
a bit slaphappy after the grind.
Someone's been trying to reach you
        all afternoon. I call
        back. My Dad's assistant
in Colorado. *Your father left NY*
for Mexico. Then he flew here.
        He jumped around noon
        from the top of
this building. Are you coming
to the funeral? I leave for
        NY. No one else
        is going out West
except a business friend Jack who
is loyal although stuck with debts.
        They tell me he
        folded his topcoat neatly
and put his felt hat alongside
before he swandived and forgot to
        float back up through
        the warm May air.

There are some silver goblets left
I take with me. I cannot look
    at his face. I
    don't want to remember
anything but my father live. The
air has a mountain clarity. It
    is beautiful there. I
    will not be alive
the same way again, without him.
I can't take that untaken trip
    to New York. He is
    with me even now.

Biographical Note

A Guggenheim fellow, Willis Barnstone has been the recipient of many awards over the years, including the NEA, the NEH, the Emily Dickinson Award of the Poetry Society of America, the W. H. Auden Award of the New York State Council on the Arts, the Midland Authors Award, four Book of the Month selections, and four Pulitzer nominations. His work has appeared in magazines including *APR*, *Harper's*, *New York Review of Books*, *Paris Review*, *Poetry*, *Nation*, *New Yorker*, and *Times Literary Supplement*.